The Journey of Odysseus

A myth from Ancient Greece

David Calcutt

Illustrated by
Carlos Lara

D1825478

CONTENTS

OXFORD
UNIVERSITY PRESS

Dear Reader,

The story of Odysseus is one of the oldest in the world. It follows the journey of the hero, Odysseus, on his way home to his wife, Penelope, after the Trojan War. The journey takes ten years and he has many adventures along the way. Danger lurks everywhere so he has to use not only his courage, but also his cunning and wit.

The story was first written down by the poet Homer, in Ancient Greece over 2500 years ago, but Odysseus' story was probably told long before then. Many other versions have since been told and written. This is my version – I hope you enjoy it!

David Calcutt

Chapter 1
The cave

**Odysseus stood at** the entrance to the cave, looking into the darkness. His men gathered around him, nervous and fearful. Behind them, the waves lapped the rim of the sandy bay where their ships were anchored.

• *Odysseus:* (say) 'uh-diss-ee-oos'.

A week had passed since they had set sail from Troy. The ten-year war was over and at last they could return home to Ithaca. They had stopped at this unknown island to find meat and to take on fresh water. With their new supplies the men were eager to head for home. It was Odysseus who had spotted the cave. 'Let's just take a quick look,' he suggested.

His men sighed but followed.

Now, standing at the mouth of the cave, they felt uneasy. Great pine and oak trees crowded round the entrance, shutting out much of the light. Odysseus parted a curtain of dark leaves and the men squinted into the gloom. The cave was huge. At the back, the embers of a fire glowed.

Odysseus turned to his men. His face was serious, but his dark eyes twinkled. 'Let's go in,' he said. 'It's only good manners to introduce ourselves.'

It was clear that someone lived there. Along the back wall were stacks of round cheeses and wooden pails. To one side was a pile of logs. Along another wall were stone pens for animals.

Odysseus stood apart from his men as he gazed around the cavern. He was small and stocky, with broad shoulders and thick-set legs. His men were lucky to have him as their leader. They could trust no one more in times of danger or hardship. But they also knew Odysseus loved an adventure. He was daring, but at times he could be reckless. This, they thought, was one of those times.

'Captain,' said Eurylochus, one of the braver men, 'there's nobody at home. Let's just take some cheeses and go back to the ship.'

Odysseus looked at him from under his dark brows. He seemed disappointed. Then he smiled. 'Right,' he said, 'but let's have something to eat and drink first.'

He held up two bags of grape juice he'd brought with him from the ship.

The men had just begun to help themselves to the cheeses when the ground began to shudder.

Slow, heavy footsteps pounded up to the cave and the bleating of goats filled the air. A dark shadow fell across the walls of the cavern. The men turned to see a monstrous figure filling the entrance.

Chapter 2
The Cyclops

The creature was three times the size of a man.
He wore a rough tunic of patched goat skins, and
one of his huge fists gripped a heavy wooden
staff. His head was covered in thick, red hair, and
the same red hair covered his shoulders, arms
and legs. His mouth was wide open, showing
many sharp and ragged teeth. In the middle of
his forehead was a single eye.

A Cyclops!

Odysseus had heard stories of these one-eyed
creatures. They were an ancient race who lived
on their island, shut off from the rest of the
world. But he had been unsure whether those
stories were true – until now.

His spirit shuddered. Some of those stories
had spoken of dark and savage deeds.

Odysseus' men stumbled in terror at the
sight of this creature and shrank into the back
of the cave.

Odysseus remained still and silent as the Cyclops let his goats into the cavern and herded them into their pens.

Then the Cyclops picked up some logs and flung them onto the fire, throwing up a shower of sparks and ash. Soon the flickering light of the flames danced around the cave. The Cyclops' single eye seemed to burn with that same light, as he peered into the gloom.

'You, men. Who are you? What are you doing here?'

'We are just simple sailors,' said cunning Odysseus. 'We lost our way trying to get home.'

A low growl came from deep in the Cyclops' chest.

'Or pirates,' he said, 'come to take what does not belong to you!' With a flick of his powerful hand, he rolled a large boulder across the entrance, blocking the way out. 'Know this,' he rasped. 'I am Polyphemus, son of the sea god, Poseidon, and now you are here, you will stay until I have done with you!'

Suddenly he reached down, grabbed two men in his huge fists, lifted them off the floor and ate them.

Odysseus and his men were frozen with horror. The Cyclops lifted one of the pails to his mouth and gulped down the milk. He settled himself on the floor beside the fire, full and content, and slept.

The men were appalled and terrified. Had they survived ten years of fighting at Troy only to die horribly in this cave? Had their great captain, Odysseus, led them to their doom? They muttered to themselves as they huddled together on the stone floor. Odysseus sat apart and said nothing. He gazed thoughtfully into the flames of the fire.

Chapter 3
Thoughts of home

Odysseus thought of home, his beloved rocky island of Ithaca. He longed to see his wife, Penelope, and Telemachus, their son. He knew he must use all his wit and cunning to free himself and his men from the Cyclops' cave, and to take them all safely home to Ithaca.

He gazed deeper into the fire. It seemed that its flames were now burning inside his head.

* * *

Within the flames he saw two figures, a woman and a boy. They were standing on a mountain-top, looking out across the sea.

His heart leapt. It was Mount Aetos! The woman standing there was Penelope, his wife, Queen of Ithaca. He recognised the white robe she was wearing, the blue, hooded cloak, her dark hair falling over it.

• *Telemachus:* (say) 'tul-em-uh-kuhss'. • *Aetos:* (say) 'ah-et-os'. **11**

Then the boy standing next to her, dressed in the goat skin tunic, must be Telemachus. He had been a baby when Odysseus had last seen him, ten years ago. He had been cradled in Penelope's arms, on the day he left for the war at Troy. Now here he was, a fine-looking boy that any father would be proud of.

As Odysseus fixed his eyes on his son, he saw the boy raise his hand and point. Then he heard his son speak.

'Mother, look!'

From one of the distant mountains across the water came a burst of flames. Odysseus saw Penelope's back stiffen. Then she too spoke.

'It is the signal,' she said to Telemachus. 'Troy has fallen. The war is over.' She smiled at her son. 'Your father is coming home.'

Those words made Odysseus' heart ache with longing. He wanted to call out to his wife and son, for them to turn their heads and see him. Yet he found he couldn't speak. The light of the flames grew dim and the figures faded. But still Odysseus heard that one word, over and over again.

Home ... home ... home ...

Chapter 4
Escape

The word *home* still echoed in Odysseus' head when he woke. It was morning. Slats of pale sunlight showed through the gaps in the blocked entrance. He gave a low moan. He was still in the cave, and the Cyclops was awake.

The creature rose to its feet, stretched, then cast its eye greedily over the sleeping men. Before Odysseus could shout a word of warning, the Cyclops reached out and snatched one of the men. That poor man was breakfast, before he was even awake! Odysseus could only look on with horror, wondering which of them would be next.

When he was finished, the Cyclops rolled away the stone from the entrance and let his goats out to graze on the mountain slopes. 'I shall return,' he growled at Odysseus before leaving the cave. 'And I shall be hungry again!' He grinned a horrible grin, then blocked the entrance again with another large stone from outside.

All day the men waited with growing dread for the monster's return. Odysseus remained apart, but deep in thought.

As evening fell, they heard the goats bleating and the monster's heavy footsteps returning. Odysseus turned to his men.

'Listen, I have a plan ...'

He had just finished talking when the Cyclops rolled away the stone and entered with his goats. All happened as before. The goats were penned, the fire built up, the stone rolled back across the entrance. Then the Cyclops licked his lips and looked at the men. He reached out.

'Wait,' shouted Odysseus. 'Before you eat, you should drink, to clear the dust out of your mouth.' He held up one of the bags of grape juice they had brought from the ship.

'Try this.'

The Cyclops took the bag from Odysseus, pulled out the stopper and sniffed.

'What is it?'

'Juice. Drink some. It's good.'

The Cyclops opened his wide mouth and poured some of the juice down his throat.

He gasped and his one eye burned bright. 'It is good!' he said, then emptied the bag, threw it aside and held out his fist. 'Give me more!'

Odysseus gave the second bag to the Cyclops. The creature drank it all in one go, unaware that Odysseus had added a special potion. He had never tasted anything like this before. It made him feel giddy and happy, but it also made him feel sleepy. He staggered and reeled about the cavern, roaring out, 'Good, good! More, more, more!' Then suddenly he stopped and peered down at Odysseus.

'Tell me your name, man,' he said.

Odysseus was too cunning to give his real name.

'My name,' he said, 'is Nobody.'

'Well, Nobody,' said the Cyclops, 'because you have given me this wonderful drink, I'm going to do you a favour. I won't eat you until I've eaten all the others!' Then he gave a great booming laugh, stumbled sideways and toppled over flat onto his back. He belched and began to snore.

Then Odysseus and his men blinded the sleeping creature with its own wooden staff.

The Cyclops woke, howling with pain. The men scattered. Once more the Cyclops staggered around the cavern, this time clutching at his wounded face. 'I'm hurt!' he screamed. 'I've been blinded! Help me, brothers! Nobody has wounded me! Nobody has blinded me!'

His fellow Cyclopes who lived nearby heard these cries, but they just thought that Polyphemus was having a bad, confused dream. They ignored him. When the Cyclops realised that his brothers weren't coming to help, the monster sank to the floor, moaning. At last, exhausted, he slept.

Odysseus and his men waited for day to come.

It was the bleating of his goats that woke the Cyclops. Still groaning with pain, he rose to his feet and felt his way around the cavern until he found the pens and let the goats out. Then he found the entrance stone. He rolled it just enough to allow one goat through at a time. He stroked the back of each goat as it passed.

'Just you wait,' he muttered into the back of the cave, where he thought the men were. 'You will pay for what you have done!'

But what the Cyclops couldn't see was that under each goat, a man was clinging on for dear life.

Once they were outside, Odysseus and his men ran back to their ship. They leapt in and began to row away, the wooden blades churning the blue water to a white foam. When they were safely offshore, Odysseus stood in the prow and called out to the Cyclops. 'Monster! Did you think you could destroy the Greeks with your brute force? You've been punished for your greed! And if you want to know who blinded you, it wasn't *Nobody*. It was *Odysseus*, the warrior, King of Ithaca!'

At this, the Cyclops gave a howl of rage and came stamping out of the cave. He gathered up the huge boulder and hurled it with all his strength in the direction of Odysseus' voice. The stone crashed into the sea, sending up a great wave that washed over the ships. The Greeks pulled hard on their oars and rowed the ships around the coast towards safety.

The Cyclops raised his arms and cried out, 'Father, Poseidon! Hear me! Call up the oceans against these men! Send your rage and wrath against them! Let Odysseus, King of Ithaca, never reach his home!'

Polyphemus' voice rang out clear. Deep in the ocean something stirred. Along the horizon the sky grew dark, as the storm clouds of the sea god began to gather.

Chapter 5
A survivor

Queen Penelope sat on her carved, wooden throne in the great hall of the palace on Ithaca. Her son, Telemachus, sat beside her. Not far away stood a young nobleman, Antinous. All watched in silence as a ragged, unkempt man sitting before them finished his meal. When he took his last gulp of milk, Penelope spoke.

'Are you finished?'

The man nodded. 'Yes, thank you, my lady,' he said. 'For now.'

Penelope raised her right hand and a servant took away the empty plate and cup. For a while she said nothing but looked intently at the man. His clothes were torn and his hair was long and knotted.

Although he'd just eaten he had a starved look. When Antinous had brought him to the palace she hadn't recognised him, but now she did. He had sailed to Troy with Odysseus years ago. Now here he was, washed up on the shore of Ithaca. It had been a long time since the war at Troy had ended. Many who had fought there had returned to their homes. She wanted to know why Odysseus hadn't. The dark-haired Queen leaned forward.

'Tell me your story,' she said.

The man looked at Penelope, then at Telemachus and Antinous. He coughed and ran his hand across his face.

'It's not a happy story, my lady,' he said.

'Never mind,' said Penelope. 'Go on.'

Chapter 6

Aeolus and the floating island

When they left the island of the Cyclops, Odysseus ordered his fleet of ships to sail northwest.

'We're a long way from home,' he said, 'and the sea god has become our enemy. Poseidon will do all he can to stop us returning home. But I think I know a way of outwitting him.'

They sailed on under dark skies and over rough seas until rising out of the gloom they saw an island. This wasn't an ordinary island. Sheer cliffs rose from the sea to the sky. On top of the cliffs were high walls of bronze that glowed in the dull light.

The most fantastic thing about this island, however, was that it wasn't fixed in one place, but floating. A walled, floating island!

'This is the home of Aeolus,' said Odysseus. 'He wanders across the world on that island of his. He's a favourite of the gods, and with his help we'll soon be in Ithaca.'

As they approached the island, two huge bronze harbour doors opened. The ships passed through. Waiting for them on the harbourside was a tall, grey-haired man wearing a flowing robe of many colours and holding a long wooden staff.

It was Aeolus.

Aeolus greeted Odysseus and his men and led them into his palace. In a great stone hall, tables and chairs were set out for a feast. Every kind of food they had dreamed of during their long hard years at Troy was there – fine white bread, creamy cheese, roast meat, honey, fruit – and all washed down with sweet juice.

They ate until they were full, then ate some more! Then they were taken to beds covered with soft woollen rugs, and fell asleep to the gentle music of flutes.

They stayed there for a whole month, feasting and sleeping. Odysseus told Aeolus the story of the war at Troy, and of their meeting with the Cyclops.

'He's a son of Poseidon,' said Odysseus. 'And because we blinded him the sea god will do everything in his power to stop us reaching Ithaca. I fear he may even destroy us. He has command over the oceans and can summon up storms to sink my ships and drown us all.'

'He can,' said Aeolus. 'But I have command

over the winds. Zeus, King of the gods, has given me that power. I will use it to help you return home safely.'

Aeolus called his oldest daughter to him. She brought a large, empty bag made of ox skin, tied with a silver cord.

She smiled at Odysseus; then the three of them climbed a steep, winding staircase that led up through the cliffs to a room at the very top of the island. The room had four high walls with a large open window in each. It was very still and quiet. Not the faintest breeze stirred the air.

'This is the Chamber of the Winds,' said Aeolus. 'They will come when I call them.' He turned to his daughter. 'Be ready,' he said.

Aeolus stood in the centre of the room and raised his staff. His daughter stood beside him and opened the bag. She held the neck wide with both hands.

Then Aeolus cried out in a voice that echoed around the chamber, and across the whole island. 'Boreas! North wind! Come!'

He struck the floor with his staff, and a booming sound echoed around the island. Then a wind came howling and rushing in through the north-facing window. It seemed so powerful that Odysseus was afraid it would sweep them all off their feet. But before he even felt it touch his face, it swept into the bag that Aeolus' daughter was holding. She closed the neck firmly.

Aeolus raised his staff again, and called out.

'Eurus! East wind! Come!'

He struck the floor and once more a wind came howling into the chamber, this time through the east-facing window. Aeolus' daughter opened the neck of the bag and caught it.

Finally, Aeolus called out,

'Notos! South wind! Come!'

The staff struck the floor and the south wind came and swirled into the bag.

The daughter pulled the silver cord tightly around the neck of the bag and laid it at Odysseus' feet.

• *Eurus:* (say) 'you-ruhss'. • *Notos:* (say) 'not-oss'. **31**

'These three winds are my gift to you, Odysseus,' said Aeolus. 'Keep them safe. Now only Zephyrus, the west wind, remains free, and that's the wind that will drive you swiftly home.'

Odysseus thanked Aeolus and lifted the bag. Although it was swollen with the three winds, it weighed almost nothing.

'Keep the bag tied until you reach Ithaca,' said Aeolus. 'And when you set the winds free, open the neck just a little, to let out each one separately. Do not set them free at the same time.'

Odysseus promised to do as Aeolus said. Then, with the bag slung across his shoulder, he returned to his ship and set sail for home.

• *Zephyrus:* (say) 'zef-ee-ruhss'.

Chapter 7
A dangerous secret

When his men asked what was in the bag,
Odysseus simply told them it was a precious
gift. He planned to surprise them all when they
reached Ithaca. For the time being, he stowed it
beneath the bench where he sat and slept.

The fleet of ships sailed out through the
bronze gates and away from the island. The west
wind filled their sails and they raced across the
ocean, flinging up showers of glittering spray
from their curved prows. The sun was bright, the
skies were clear. Soon the men recognised the
seas they were sailing through. One evening, just
as the sun was sinking beneath the waves, they
smelled land.

'We'll see Ithaca with the next sun's rising,' said Odysseus happily. He settled down to sleep. It was a clear night, with a bright, full moon.

As he slept, his men began to talk about the mysterious bag. They were itching with curiosity. Some of them didn't trust their cunning captain.

'You know what he's like,' said one. 'It could be treasure, and he wants to keep it all for himself.'

'If it is, we should all have a share,' said another.

'It might not be treasure,' said Eurylochus.

'What else could it be?' said another of the men. 'Why else would he keep it hidden away under his bench?'

'He doesn't want us to get our hands on it.'

'There's only one way to settle it. Let's take a look.'

'Hang on,' said Eurylochus. 'I don't think we should do that.'

'You're outvoted, Eurylochus,' said the first man. 'Come on, lads.'

The men crept to where Odysseus lay sleeping.

The first man reached under the bench and drew out the ox-skin bag. The others gathered round as he loosened the silver cord. They peered over his shoulder.

WHOOOOOSH!

The three winds came ripping and roaring out of the bag. They swirled about with such force that the men were swept off their feet, flung high into the air and hurled screaming into the sea. The winds twisted and whirled around the ships; all four of them now – north, south, east and west battling together, whipping the waves into a frenzied storm.

Beneath the ocean, Poseidon, the sea god laughed. He ordered the storm to rage wilder and fiercer. Fists of dark cloud knotted in the sky. Lightning flashed, thunder cracked. The winds shrieked like mad birds and tore down upon the ships, splintering their masts, ripping their sides, so that their planks burst and seawater poured in. Pounded by the piling, driving waves, the ships were thrown apart.

The fleet scattered across the wide and storm-wrecked sea.

Chapter 8
Dead or alive?

In the palace on Ithaca, Penelope and the others listened as the man finished his story. 'I fear all the ships were lost in that storm,' he said. 'None could have survived.'

'But you did,' said Penelope.

The man looked at the floor. 'I was one of those who opened the bag,' he said. 'I was flung with the others into the sea. I found a piece of wreckage and clung to it and the waves brought me to Ithaca. The gods must have let me live so that I could return to tell the tale.'

'And be punished for your foolishness,' growled the nobleman, Antinous.

'No,' said Penelope. 'The man has suffered enough.' She spoke to her servants. 'Give him fresh clothing,' she said. 'Then let him return to his home and family.'

After the man had gone, Antinous turned to Penelope.

'This is dreadful news,' he said. 'I am sorry to hear it. It is sad for us to have lost a king, and sad for you to have lost a husband, and for Telemachus to have lost a father.'

Telemachus jumped to his feet, his dark eyes blazing.

'My father is not dead!' he shouted.

'It is difficult for the boy to understand,' said Antinous, 'but you must, Queen Penelope. You understand that Ithaca needs a king. So, you must think of marrying again.'

Now Penelope's eyes blazed like her son's.

'No,' she said. 'I shall not think of it. Telemachus spoke the truth. Odysseus is not dead. I know it. Though he may be lost, he shall return. And he'll find his wife and son waiting for him.'

Then, with Telemachus at her side, she walked out of the throne-room.

Antinous watched them go. Then he walked across to Odysseus' great throne, next to Penelope's, and stared at them both, deep in thought.

Chapter 9

Enchanted islands

Odysseus sailed on, through calm waters now.
Alone of all the ships, his had survived the
terrible storm. The warring winds, however, had
blown his ship far from Ithaca into strange and
unknown seas. Now he stood at the prow, gazing
towards the horizon, wondering what new trials
and dangers awaited him. Whatever they were,
he was ready to face them.

Over the next few months, Odysseus sailed on, stopping at islands to forage for food and fresh water. On one island they lost two of their crew to savage cannibals. On another, the men ate a sweet smelling plant which caused them to fall into an enchanted sleep.

The next island they came to was the home of the goddess Circe, daughter of the sun. She was no friend to men, and any who came to her island she turned into animals with her magic staff. She did the same to Odysseus' men, but Odysseus snapped her magic staff, and the spell was broken. Circe knew she had met her match and begged Odysseus to stay.

Odysseus did stay for a while, but thoughts of home eventually returned. He grew sad and anxious. How could they ever find their way out of these strange waters and reach Ithaca? Circe took pity on Odysseus and told him that there was only one man who could answer that question – Tiresias, the blind prophet.

'Tiresias?' said Odysseus. 'How can he tell us anything? He died long ago.'

'You can still speak with him,' said Circe. 'But you must travel to where his spirit dwells now. You must seek him in the Land of the Dead.'

Chapter 10

The Land of the Dead

The sea was flat and still. Nothing moved. Ahead of Odysseus' ship lay a dark shore, lined with black, leafless trees. The men dipped their oars into the dull water and the ship moved slowly forwards until it touched the shore. All was silent. The men sat silent, too. They had sailed to the very edge of the world and had now come to the Land of the Dead. A cold terror gripped each man's heart.

Odysseus was standing near the prow, gazing into the dead land. He turned and spoke to his men. His voice sounded flat and his words dropped like hard pebbles onto the deck.

'Stay here, men. I'll go alone. Wait here until I return.'

As he jumped from the ship and waded ashore, each man had the same thought: 'What if he doesn't?'

Odysseus had the same thought, too.

The terror that gripped his men's hearts gripped
his own, but he would not show it. He stood
grim and alert on that silent, pale-lit shore,
waiting for the dead to appear. He would not
show them his fear.

For a long time there was nothing. Then there came a soft, dry whispering, like the sound of autumn leaves blowing across the path. From behind the leafless trees, wisps of smoke or mist appeared, drifting through the gloom towards him. As they drew closer Odysseus saw that they had human forms. They were pale and colourless, and it was their voices he could hear whispering. Soon they gathered around him. Their faces were close but they had a distant look, as if they were peering up from the bed of some deep, cold river.

Odysseus shivered. As he gazed from one face to another, he realised that he recognised many – they were faces he had known at Troy, warriors who had been killed in the many battles fought there. Among them was the great Achilles, best of the Greek warriors, who had fallen just a few months before they had taken the city. When Odysseus saw him, he gasped his name, but Achilles turned away and moved back towards the trees.

'Achilles!' Odysseus called. 'Don't you know me?'

Achilles stopped and turned back. Odysseus saw great sorrow and bitterness in the warrior's eyes.

'I know you, Odysseus,' said the sad spirit. 'And I know that you still live in the world of light, while I must dwell here, where all is mist and shadow.'

'But your fame lives on in that world,' said Odysseus. 'Your deeds and your name will be remembered there forever.'

'I would rather be a poor farmer,' said Achilles, 'or even a slave, and walk in the sunlight, than have fame here in the kingdom of the dead.'

Then he turned away and was lost in the shadows.

Many other spirits still crowded round Odysseus, with their misty bodies, pale faces and dry, whispering voices. When Odysseus spoke again, his voice rang out loud and echoed along the gloomy shore.

'I am Odysseus. I seek the prophet Tiresias. Where is he?'

A voice spoke softly, but clearly.

'Here.'

The spirits drew back to reveal a figure standing beneath one of the black trees. It was an old man, wearing a ragged, grey cloak. His hair and beard were white and the eyes that stared unblinking out of his face were sightless. Even so, the old man came walking towards Odysseus.

'I am Tiresias. Why do you seek me here?'

'I want to find my way home,' said Odysseus. 'I believe you can help me.'

Tiresias bowed his head for a moment. When he raised it, his eyes seemed to be peering into the future. 'Many dangers await you on your journey home,' said Tiresias. 'A terrible whirlpool will try to drag you down beneath the waves. You will pass Scylla, the many-headed monster, who feasts on those who sail too near her rock. The Sirens, with their feathers and claws of birds, will try to lure you and your men to your death with their singing.'

'With luck and judgement you'll survive. But

when you are almost home you will come to the island of the sun god. You will be tired and hungry and will need to rest there, find food and take on fresh water. Be warned. The sun god keeps his cattle on that island. If just one of these is harmed, your good luck will leave you. The sun will leave the skies, and a terrible storm will smash your ship and send it plunging down deep into the ocean.'

The blind prophet said no more. He turned to go.

'Wait,' said Odysseus. 'There's one more thing I want to know.'

Tiresias gave a sharp hiss that wrapped itself around Odysseus like a cold-skinned snake. He shivered.

'Be quick,' the prophet whispered. 'It tires us to stand here at the world's edge. You called us and keep us. We long to return to the shadow world below.'

'Tell me how things are on Ithaca,' said Odysseus. 'My wife, Penelope. My son,

Telemachus. Is all well with them?'

This time Tiresias did not speak. Or if he did, Odysseus did not hear his voice. But he saw a vision in the prophet's eyes.

Chapter 11
The vision

The great hall in the palace of Ithaca was filled
with men. They were feasting and the hall rang
with their laughter and loud voices. Standing
apart, against the wall, stood a handsome,
dark-haired youth. His arms were folded across
his chest and he glared with angry, sullen eyes
at the feasting men.

One of the feasters, a young nobleman dressed
in a fine cloak and tunic, called across to the
youth.

'Telemachus! Come and join us! Drink a toast
in memory of your father!'

The man sitting next to him spoke up.

'And thank his spirit for providing us with such
a fine feast.'

'Today, and every day!' said a third man. They
all roared with laughter and beat their fists on
the tables.

Telemachus unfolded his arms and walked

towards the nobleman. The flame of anger flashed in his dark eyes.

'I won't drink with you, Antinous, nor with any of this rabble who defile my mother's home.'

The men's laughter died on their lips. Silence swept through the hall. Everyone stared at Antinous and Telemachus.

'You should be more respectful of your elders, boy,' said Antinous. He stood up and walked over to Telemachus, his eyes never leaving the boy's. 'Especially as one of them may soon be your new father.'

'As soon as your mother makes up her mind which one it will be,' said one of the men.

'I have a father,' said Telemachus.

'Yes, you do,' called out another of the men. 'He's feeding with the fishes at the bottom of the sea!'

Telemachus' face flushed with shame and rage and he clenched his fists.

'Careful, boy,' said Antinous, in a low voice. 'You might hurt yourself.'

At that moment, a woman's voice called out from above.

'What is all this noise?'

Silence fell again. Queen Penelope stood on the balcony above.

'Have you no shame, you men?' she said. 'Not only do you eat our food, but you fill the halls of my palace with your noise and riot!'

Antinous spoke to her, smiling.

'We shall leave you in peace, lady, when you have chosen one of us to be your husband. Until then we shall stay as guests in your house.'

'Then you must stay,' said Penelope, 'until the man returns who will send you home – or to the halls of death!'

Her words rang out across the hall. Every man shivered as if an icy wind blew through the palace. Then the dark-haired Queen turned, walked back into her room and closed the door.

* * *

Odysseus shivered too, as the vision faded. He blinked and looked about him. The spirits had gone. He stood alone on the dark shore of the dead land.

He felt uneasy. In the vision, his son was almost grown, yet it was just a few months ago that Odysseus had left Troy and Telemachus was only ten years old. Had Tiresias granted him a glimpse of the future? Was he doomed never to return, to be lost at sea, or to wander the world's oceans forever?

He turned and waded back through the water

and climbed aboard his ship. His men crowded round him.

'Did you see Tiresias?'

'What did he tell you?'

'What other dangers await us?'

'Will we overcome them?'

'We will get home, won't we?'

Odysseus put on his bravest face and his broadest grin. He spoke in his biggest voice.

'Yes,' he said, 'there are dangers awaiting us. Yes, we'll overcome them – and yes, we'll get back home. We're Greeks, men, and we're Ithacans. Nothing will keep us from returning to our land.'

With their hearts cheered by Odysseus' words, his men took to the oars and rowed away from the dead land. They made their way out of that silent, sunless sea, and into the world of waves and wind and light.

Only Odysseus' heart remained heavy. He was filled with a sense of dread at what he had seen.

Chapter 12
The shroud

Penelope stood at the window in her room,
gazing out across the sea. Every day she stood
here looking for a sail to appear on the horizon,
looking out for Odysseus returning home.

Today, as every day, no sail appeared.

Cries, shouts and cheers rose from the
courtyard below. The noblemen of Ithaca
were holding games – wrestling, spear-
throwing, racing – to pass the time before their
evening meal.

They did this almost every day. Many suitors were gathered, each hoping that the dark-haired Queen would choose him to be her new husband, and the new King of Ithaca. The laws of hospitality meant she could not turn them away.

So they stayed, eating, drinking, filling the palace with their noise. They refused to leave until she made her choice.

They all believed that Odysseus was dead.

'After so many years, he must be,' they said. Penelope didn't believe it. She knew her husband was still alive. She knew that one day he would return. But until then, what was she to do? She feared not only for herself but for Telemachus. He was growing now, almost a man. The suitors knew how much he hated them. One day his temper might get the better of him, and he would do something rash. Someone like Antinous would be only too pleased to have an excuse to kill him.

Things were becoming more and more difficult.

The door opened. It was Odysseus' father, Laertes. He lived alone on the other side of the island. Since the suitors had come, he rarely visited the palace.

'I've come to ask you a favour,' he said to Penelope. 'I've had a dream. In the dream I died but could not be buried, because there was no shroud to wrap my body in.'

'You're a long time yet from dying,' said Penelope.

'Even so,' said Laertes, 'I won't feel at ease until I know I have a shroud. I would like you to weave one for me.'

Penelope bowed her head. 'I'll gladly do that for you,' she said.

Laertes thanked her, then left. Penelope watched him from the window as he walked away. He was a good man and deserved the finest work. She would take a long time over making the shroud.

Then her eyes flashed and she sat up in her chair. A smile came to her lips. Once more she gazed across the island to where the sea glittered in the sunlight. The idea glittered too, hard and bright and strong in her mind. She would tell her suitors that she would choose a husband once she had finished making the shroud for Laertes. But what she wouldn't tell them was that she would unmake it each night, so the shroud would never be finished. That should keep the suitors at bay until Odysseus finally returned.

Chapter 13

The Scylla and the Sirens

The sea churned and writhed and boiled. It swirled round and round. As the ship drew close to the whirlpool's edge the men could feel it pulling at the timbers. It was as if some creature had its claws clamped fast and was trying to drag them towards its dark, gaping centre.

'Pull hard to the left!' roared Odysseus. The men on the port side heaved at their oars, muscles straining, arms and backs aching and burning with effort. Slowly, the ship moved clear of the whirlpool and the waters grew calmer. Odysseus lowered his voice. 'Steady now,' he said. 'We're not clear of danger yet.'

63

To their left, jagged black rocks rose high above them, clawing at the air like cracked fingers. The waves churned about them, flinging up mist and spray. Among these rocks slept the sea monster, Scylla. In order to steer clear of the whirlpool, the ship had to pass close to these rocks. They risked waking the monster.

'Slow and easy,' said Odysseus. 'Pull gently, lads, and we'll make it through safe and sound.'

The men raised and dipped and pulled on the oars as slowly as they could. The helmsman gripped the tiller with both hands, trying to hold it steady. It seemed as if they would succeed, when a sudden and strong wave buffeted the ship. It lurched to the left, scraping the edge of the last rock.

That was enough to wake Scylla. With a roar she reared up from the rocks, her many long necks writhing and twisting like snakes. The jaws in her heads yawned wide, their teeth bared. From deep within her body came a sound like the howling of a pack of hungry hounds.

'Quickly, now!' yelled Odysseus. 'Hard on those oars, lads!'

The ship leaped forward through the waves, speeding away from the rocks. But one of Scylla's long necks lunged downwards. The mouth widened, and the jaws snapped at the poor helmsman. The men stared in horror as they saw their comrade dragged off the ship. It was horrible, but there was no time for pity.

The ocean lay calm ahead of them. The men rested at their oars and let the wind in the sail drive the ship onwards. It was a warm day and soon the men were asleep, exhausted by their adventures.

Odysseus let them rest. He stood with his hand resting lightly on the tiller, guiding the ship through the rest of the day and on through the night.

Odysseus ran the length of the deck, grabbed the tiller and guided the ship away from danger.

In the morning, Odysseus roused his men. Fresh danger was approaching. Ahead of them lay a small, rocky island, the island of the Sirens. The song of these bird-faced women could drive men mad and send them plunging overboard to their deaths.

Odysseus told his men to plug their ears with wax, so that they could hear nothing. As for himself, the wily sea captain commanded his men to bind him to the mast with strong ropes.

He wanted to be the only man in the world to hear the Sirens' song and survive.

That's just what happened. The wild, beautiful, terrible, deadly song of the Sirens sent Odysseus into a frenzy. He tried to tear himself free of his bonds and fling himself into the waves, but he could not break free. As they passed the island, his madness left him.

Chapter 14
Temptation

He had survived.

The ship sailed on and at last came to the island of Helios, the sun god. It was a green, pleasant island, watered by many streams and pools. There were olive groves and fruit trees, and meadows of long, sweet grass. Grazing in these meadows were the red-coated, long-horned cattle of the sun. Odysseus told his men to gather as much fruit and olives as they could and to fill their barrels with fresh water.

'We're not far from home, now,' said Odysseus. 'What we take on here should see us back.'

He had already warned them not to touch the cattle of the sun god. He reminded them again as they left the ship and waded through the shallows to the shore.

'Just fruit and olives for now,' he called after them. 'You can have all the meat you want once we're in Ithaca.'

Then he lay down on his bench at the front of the ship and covered himself with his cloak. For the first time in many days, he slept.

Odysseus woke later to the smell of freshly cooked meat.

He leaped to his feet and stared in horror at the shore. There were his men, gathered around a huge fire. Over the fire a cow was roasting on a wooden spit. But he couldn't bring himself to be angry, when he saw how thin and hungry his men looked.

The temptation had been too strong.

Odysseus let them eat their fill, then cast off and set sail for home. He could only hope that the sun god wouldn't notice that one of his cattle had been killed.

The sun god did notice, and he was angry. Odysseus' ship had hardly begun to sail away when the sky shook with a deep, ringing boom, as if a great gong had been struck. Dark clouds rolled across the sun. Then a howling wind sprang up, the ocean heaved and the waves piled high and came toppling down like mountains upon the ship. Its mast splintered and fell. Its timbers cracked. Its deck split wide and the sea water poured in.

Deep down on the sea bed Poseidon laughed. At last he would have his revenge for the blinding of his son.

The storm did not last long, but the ship was lost forever beneath the wide, rolling ocean. All its crew were lost, save one. Odysseus clung to a piece of broken timber, drifting on the waves under the burning sun, as far from home as he had ever been.

At last the sea currents washed him ashore another unknown island. There he was found by the sea nymph, Calypso. She nursed him back to health, but refused to let him leave. She used her magic to keep him there for seven years.

Every day Odysseus went to the shore and began to build a raft, so he could set out for home. Every day Calypso used her magic to ensure the raft was never finished. The next morning Odysseus would find the raft broken to pieces on the sand. Even though it seemed a helpless task, he never gave up. If he did, it would mean giving up hope of returning to Ithaca, and he would never do that.

Early one morning, as Odysseus knelt in the sand among the scattered timbers and prepared to begin building again, a strange light shimmered over the sea. For a moment it just hung there, a glimmer of gold in the red light of morning.

Then suddenly it began to move, racing over the wave tops, rushing at a terrific speed towards the island. The next thing Odysseus knew it was there on the beach, and the whole shore was filled with golden light, making his skin tingle and the air sing. He was in the presence of a god. It was Hermes, the messenger.

'Build your raft, Odysseus,' said Hermes. 'It will not be broken again. Calypso's magic has been taken from her. It is time for you to return home.'

'Home!' said Odysseus. 'Then my sufferings are over at last.'

'Not quite,' said Hermes. 'Danger awaits you on Ithaca. Be on your guard when you return.'

Then the light faded and was gone but hope

stirred once more in Odysseus' weary heart.

That day he finished building the raft. He said farewell to Calypso and set off alone on the sea to Ithaca.

Chapter 15
The beggar

The suitors were gathered as usual for their evening feast. Penelope watched them from the balcony. The same faces, the same loud voices and laughter. They had grown more unruly, too, ever since they had discovered her trick with the shroud. It was one of her own servant girls who had betrayed her.

'A very clever plan, lady,' Antinous had said to her. 'You had us fooled for a while, but you'll make fools of us no more. The sooner you choose a husband, the better it will be for all of us. Until then, we will continue to make ourselves comfortable here.'

Then he had smiled a cunning smile and walked away. Penelope had learned over the years to hate that smile. She had even grown to hate the palace. It was no longer her home. It was a prison.

She was about to go back inside her room

when something caught her eye. Or rather,
someone. Set apart from the rest of the tables,
in a corner of the hall, there was a small table,
with two people sitting at it. One was her son,
Telemachus, but the other was a man she had
not seen before. From his stained and ragged
tunic, and his tangled hair and beard, he looked
to be some poor traveller.

Perhaps he was down on his luck and had
come to beg scraps and a bed for the night.
Telemachus, with his generous nature, had
brought the man in. He had food and drink set

out for him. It did, however, seem a little strange that he should be sitting at the table with the beggar, sharing a dish with him. The two men were talking with their heads bent together.

Antinous noticed this as well. He called across the hall.

'Telemachus! What are you doing sharing a table with that ruffian? A young nobleman like you shouldn't be eating with the likes of him.'

'The King's son and the beggar,' said another man. 'They make a good pair.'

'It's a disgrace to allow such louts into the palace at all,' said a third man. 'He should be outside sharing the yard with the dogs.'

Then he picked up an empty wooden bowl and flung it across the room. It struck the beggar on the shoulder.

'Good shot!' said Antinous and everyone laughed. Telemachus sprang to his feet. Penelope could see the fury in his face and her heart filled with fear for him. Although he was grown and had his father's courage, he was no match on his own against all these noblemen. Before he could speak, though, the beggar raised his hand and touched Telemachus on the arm. Telemachus looked down. The beggar said something, shook his head and Telemachus sat again, his shoulders hunched forward across the table.

The suitors laughed again, then went on with their feasting.

Penelope gazed for a moment or two longer

at this ragged traveller. She was curious about him. She wanted to ask Telemachus what he knew about him, and why he was sharing his food and talking with him. Was he more than he seemed? She turned and went back into her room, determined to find out more about this mysterious stranger.

Telemachus came to see her later on that evening. What he said to her drove all thoughts of the beggar out of her head.

'Mother,' said her son, 'things can't go on like this. Tomorrow I want you to call the suitors together and announce that you are ready to choose a husband.'

Penelope was so stunned that she couldn't speak.

'Tell them there will be a contest,' he went on. 'Each man will try to string and draw my father's bow. The man who does will be your husband.'

The bow was a prized possession of Odysseus'. It had been given to him by a friend when he was a young man and was a powerful weapon.

Odysseus only used it for hunting. He had not taken it to Troy. The bow was kept locked in a small room off the main hall. No one had touched it since he'd gone away.

'Your father is the only man strong enough to draw that bow,' Penelope said.

'We shall see,' said Telemachus. Then he leaned forward and took his mother's hand. 'Trust me, Mother. Tomorrow, my father's bow shall be drawn and its arrows fired – and you shall find your husband.'

There was a twinkling light in his eyes. Penelope was sure that he knew more than he was telling her. She caught a sense of excitement too, though she didn't know why. After Telemachus had gone she sat for a long time in the gathering dark. Many thoughts ran through her mind, but chiefly the thought of that ragged beggar in the hall.

Chapter 16
The final test

The next evening Penelope took Odysseus' bow and arrows into the hall. The suitors were all gathered there. Telemachus had dug a trench in the earthen floor running the length of the hall. In the trench he placed twelve tall axes in a row. Each double axe head was topped with a wide ring. When he had fixed the last axe in place he spoke to the suitors.

'Let each of you in turn take the bow, attempt to string it, and fire an arrow through the rings of these axes. The man who succeeds is my mother's husband, my father and King of Ithaca.'

Penelope handed the bow and the quiver of
arrows to Telemachus.

'Go and watch from the balcony, Mother,'
Telemachus said. Then he lowered his voice. 'It
may not be safe for you here.'

Once more there was that excited light in his eyes. Without a word, Penelope crossed the hall to the stairs that led to the balcony. As she did, she saw that there was someone else in the hall, a figure sitting on a wooden stool in one of the far corners.

He was slouched forward, dressed in tattered clothing with a ragged hood pulled over his head.

The beggar from the day before! Penelope gave a start of surprise, then carried on walking to the stairs.

She wasn't the only one to notice the stranger. As Penelope began to climb to the balcony, she heard Antinous cry out.

'Look! Who let that ruffian in?'

The others joined in.

'What's he doing here?'

'It's a disgrace!'

'Get rid of him!'

'Throw him out!'

'No!' said Telemachus. His voice rang out clear in the hall, silencing all the others. Penelope smiled when she heard it. 'This man is my guest, in my house,' he went on. 'I have asked him to stay, to witness the contest and to see that all's fair.'

'Let him stay, then, for now,' growled Antinous. 'It will be different when the contest is over and a proper man rules here.'

Then the contest began.

The first man came forward and took the bow from Telemachus. He tried to bend the bow so that he could fit the loose string into the notch at the top, but he couldn't. He gave up and handed it to the next man. He tried, he too failed.

One after another the suitors tried to string the bow. One after another they failed.

The last to take the bow was Antinous, and though he strained and pushed with all his might, he too failed. He flung the bow down angrily.

'It's impossible!' he cried, and turned to Telemachus. 'You're trying to trick us with this contest! Make fools of us! There's no man in this hall can bend this bow!'

'Let me try.'

The voice came from the back of the hall. Everyone looked. It was the beggar who had spoken. Now he rose from his seat and came slowly towards them, shuffling, limping.

'I'm not taking part in the contest,' he said,

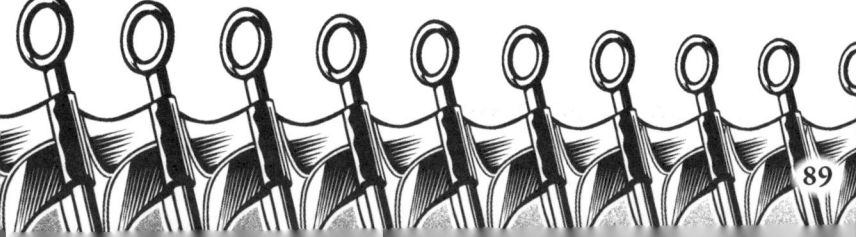

'but I'd like to see if I have the strength to bend this bow. I used to be a good archer when I was younger.'

The suitors began to cry out in protest, but Telemachus silenced them. 'What harm can it do?' he said. 'Surely you don't believe this beggar can really bend my father's bow?'

By now the beggar was standing at his side. Telemachus handed him the bow. The beggar held it up and looked at it. Then, standing it on one end, and grasping it firmly at the other, he bent it and fixed the string. The suitors gaped. None of them could speak.

The beggar snapped at the taut string with
his finger and it gave off a note that sounded
through the hall. While it was still echoing, he
took an arrow from Telemachus, fitted it to the
string, raised the bow, took aim and fired.

Once more the plucked string sounded its note.
The arrow flew through the rings and fixed in
the far wall, quivering.

The beggar raised the bow aloft and turned to

the suitors.

'I haven't lost my touch, it seems,' he said, 'And I'm a better man than all of you.' He took another arrow from the quiver, fitted it to the bow. 'Yes, indeed. I think I am the best man here.'

Suddenly his voice was not the cracked and rasping voice of the beggar. It rang out loud and deep and clear. The beggar himself seemed to grow in stature. He seemed to be lit by a strange, unearthly light.

Then he threw back his hood and cast off his rags. There before them, in cloak and tunic, stood Odysseus.

The suitors stood wide-eyed and open-mouthed, in terror. Odysseus grinned.

'You men!' he said, 'For years you've feasted in my hall, taken over my home, tried to force my wife to marry one of you. You thought I'd never return, but now I'm here, and now it's time for you to pay!'

He drew the bowstring back. Antinous reached for his sword. Odysseus let the arrow fly.

Antinous fell without a sound. His sword clattered on the floor.

For a moment there was silence, then the hall erupted in riot. Some of the suitors made ready to fight, others ran to the doors to escape. But the doors were locked. They were forced to turn back and join the others. They stood and faced Odysseus and Telemachus, calling out to each other.

'Get ready!'

'It's only two.'

'An old man and a boy.'

'We'll make short work of them.'

'Come on!'

Then they rushed forwards into the fight. It didn't last long. And at the end of it all the suitors were dead.

So Odysseus was reunited with his family. The fallen men were taken away and returned to their families for burial. Order was restored to the palace.

Odysseus had endured many troubles and hardships on his wanderings. Penelope and Telemachus had endured them too, on Ithaca. But now their troubles were over. Peace came to Ithaca, for Odysseus had returned home at last.